True Feathers

Carolyn Patrick

Susan,
Thank you for your support and your dedication to helping Veterans. I cant wait to read your book! Best of luck in writing.

Carolyn

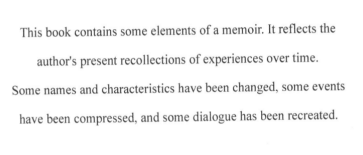

This book contains some elements of a memoir. It reflects the author's present recollections of experiences over time. Some names and characteristics have been changed, some events have been compressed, and some dialogue has been recreated.

CONTENTS

This book is dedicated to my wingman Claw and our daughter Elleanor for making me a better person with their love.

Acknowledgments

I am forever grateful to Mr. Hadi, my Iraqi counterpart and translator during Operation Iraqi Freedom in 2005, for teaching me about peace in the midst of war. Assalamu alaikum Abu Ali.

To my friends who read early versions of this story and encouraged me to keep writing, thank you for your kindness.

With gratitude to Mariya Prytula for her sage advice and beautiful artwork which captured my vision for this book.

To scholars Dr J.W. Pennebaker, Dr Van Der Kolk and Dr Richard Miller; thank you for using your talents to ease the world's suffering and bring peace to those who seek it. Your books helped me navigate through my darkest hours.

My inspiration and appreciation for nature is shared with my sister Jan who taught me to connect with the earth and pay attention to the tiniest of creatures. Thank you for being my friend and sister.

To my first yoga instructor, Kanani, and all my teachers who followed, your passion for sharing the ancient teachings of yoga brought me peace and a deeper connection to the world in which we live. The light in me honors the light in you.

To the men and women of the US Military, thank you for giving me the courage to do much more than I ever dreamed possible. Our connection continues even after we leave the military and I am buoyed by the Veteran community in organizations such as USVAA who seek to address issues of concern to veterans and their families via artistic endeavors and platforms.

A portion of the proceeds from this book will be donated to Warriors at Ease, a non-profit organization seeking to increase awareness about the power of yoga and meditation through programs that support the health and healing of service members, veterans, and their families.

FOREWORD

Thomas Paine wrote, "If there must be trouble, let it be in my day, that my child may have peace." I first read that as a cadet at Culver Military Academy, long before I had children, but to this day, it is my silent inward prayer.

I've spent most of my life as a hawk—a warrior—ready to go where commanded to do what was needed to fight for that in which I believed. Even now, fifteen years after taking off the nation's uniform for the last time, I keep my talons sharp and at the ready, my eyes always scanning for threats. It is, as they say, the nature of the beast—a price many of us pay for having done the things we've done... and seen the things we've seen. For many, that price becomes very burdensome; for some, too burdensome.

I came up through the same regimented system as Carolyn, and, of course, a few of my experiences were remarkably similar... but most, because of where we came from, who we were, and how we saw things—and how others saw us—were so very different.

Over the years, I devoured books on history, politics, leadership, management, strategy, and tactics. Looking back, I expected everyone in uniform to have the same drive, the same commitment, and the same values I had; and I was taken aback, perplexed, when they did not. I had little time and tolerance for "feelings". I didn't care about your color, creed, or where you came from. We were one team; one fight. As long as you were an effective member of that team —a hawk—we were good. Your personal problems only mattered, really, if they got in the way of the mission. Had *this* book been written then, I can assure you, to my shame, I would not have read it.

And, since I know me better than anyone, that's exactly why you should.

Human Nature is a quirky thing. Despite our "civilized" nature, we are, at our basest, hardwired for tribalism and survival. All too often, we give those things too much import, and, worse, out of ignorance, prejudice, or malice, we conflate the two. The *Us vs. Them* we are assaulted with at every turn is sad evidence of that. And yet, the Human Spirit drives us to accomplish great things, to see beyond current boundaries, and to strive for... better.

Carolyn gives me hope that the Human Spirit will overcome our Human Nature. Her story is rich with symbolism and, for those who've "been there," richer still with personal meaning that *will* touch you. *Please* read her preface, for therein lie keys to greater understanding you will otherwise, sadly, miss.

I remain, to some extent, an idealist, but I know there is no end to trouble; that it will always be a part of life. We will always need hawks... and we will always need doves.

Mark E. Bracich, Colonel, USAF (Retired)
Screenwriter, Actor, Filmmaker

PREFACE

If veterans can achieve awareness, transformation, understanding, and peace, they can share with the rest of society the realities of war. And they can teach us how to make peace with ourselves and each other, so we never have to use violence to resolve conflicts again.

Zen Master Thich Nhat Hahn

There comes a time when we all transition from warrior to veteran, and my time was near. Next week I would take my last fitness test in the Air Force and I was determined to get a personal record on my final run. Running had always been hard for me, but when I dedicated my run to one of the fallen, they would give me the push I needed to excel. This workout was for Jessica; she was mischievous but also full of life, light and laughter. She loved her son and her dogs. She served honorably through Operations Desert Storm, Iraqi Freedom and Enduring Freedom but her service had taken a toll on her health toward the end

of her career.

After a couple quick stretches on the front porch, I

started off on my run, slow and stiff. I thought about

the text message I received from Dawn last month.

*Hey, do you remember Jessica? She was in
our squadron back in Albuquerque.*

> *Sure, she retired and lives just down the road from
> me. I haven't seen her in years though, what has
> she been up to?*

*She started drinking again. I had been checking
on her and taking her to appointments when
she needed it, but I didn't hear from her for a
few days, and when I went to check on her she
was dead. I hate that she died all alone. Her
dogs were there, guarding her body…my heart
is broken.*

She loved Jessica like a sister and my heart ached

for her. I got the details for the memorial service and

told her I would be there. Dawn and I weren't close

friends but we had been through some things together.

People were drawn to her and it seemed to me she was always surrounded by friends. I was never able to connect with people the way she did, and I respected the hell out of her for it.

The funeral was small. Her family on one side of the chapel, and those who served with her on the other side of the aisle. There were a lot more of us than there was family. I took a seat with the other warriors and laid a hand on Dawn's shoulder. Usually bubbly, fun and animated, she had fallen into a pool of guilt and grief. I recognized Jessica's best friend from our assignment together; I wanted to say something to make her pain go away but I couldn't. I felt numb like I had every other time I had been called to witness death.

I turned the corner for the final stretch of my run and sprinted to the finish. It was late September, but still hot and muggy, so I took a cool down lap, determined to leave my grief on the road. Back at the house, I stopped just inside the front door and kicked off my shoes without unlacing them. Claw was sitting at his desk and I blew him a noisy kiss. When he looked up at me, I could see something was wrong. My stomach did a little flip.

"Hey there, what's up?" I asked in my best cheerful voice.

"Patch is gone. We're not sure what happened, but they found him in his apartment with a gunshot wound to the head last night."

"Oh, no." I walked over, sat in his lap, and let him hug me. His body was rigid as he tried to control his rage at losing another brother.

"Sorry, I'm all sweaty." I said and tried to pull away, but he gripped me tighter.

"I don't care," his voice cracked and the tears broke free, caught by the fabric of my already damp shirt.

Our arms wrapped tightly around each other. Our chests pressed together so our hearts could talk. I sighed, sat up a little taller and rested my chin on top of his head. I would stay like this as long as he needed me, but I let my mind slip away to the first night I met Patch at the officer's club in Okinawa.

He was a cocky young captain boasting about being the best pilot in the Air Force. The basement of the club was filled with the world's best pilots. Claw and I were having a few drinks following the dining-in ceremony, and we were still in our formal mess dress uniforms, the military version of a tuxedo. It was an Air Force tradition following formal events to allow a more relaxed version of the uniform. Our jackets would come off to reveal everyone's "party

shirts." Most of us had them made at Mr. Kim's

Custom Tailor shop in Korea. You could bring him

any material or design, and he would produce what

looked like a normal white tuxedo shirt when wearing

the jacket, but the sleeves and shirt backs would

reveal the wearer's true personality. Hawaiian prints,

patriotic flags, and vibrant team colors began to

replace the sea of blue, reminiscent of peacocks

spreading their tail feathers.

"Hey, Patch. Show my wife the back of your

shirt." Claw shouted to the table across from us.

Patch turned his back to me, flexing his arms like

a bodybuilder. Embroidered at the center was an

HH-60 with a hoist disappearing from the helicopter

down into his pants. I giggled as I read "Rescue! We

will pull you out of anywhere."

This is the way I wanted to remember him--loud and proud with a brilliant life ahead of him. The amazing men and women we danced with that night would go on to fly lifesaving missions in Korea, Afghanistan, Iraq, and even in the skies above our own country during relief efforts for hurricanes Katrina and Rita. The rest of Patch's story and the pain leading up to his demise, I will probably never know. Air Force Rescue was a small and tight-knit community with a heroic heritage united by the motto, "These things we do that others may live." This loss would hit them hard.

In the weeks following Patch's death, the news and social media seemed to bombard us with statistics of the high rates of suicide among veterans. Twenty-two a day, who would be next? Would it be the Master Sergeant juggling three kids, an out-of-work husband, and an upcoming assignment to Turkey? Or the hard-charging Major struggling with secrets he fears will ruin him? Maybe the guy with the Vietnam Vet ball cap I see every payday stocking up on whiskey at the class six? Would it be me?

With morbid curiosity, I wanted to know what we all had in common that made us so vulnerable to this killer. We all served our country. We were strong and brave, respected for the sacrifices we made. We were family—brothers and sisters in arms. We shared a unique culture and the core values of integrity first, service before self, and excellence in all we would do. We were fearless when we would arrive in a strange town, knowing we had each other's backs, reciting bases where we had been stationed when meeting new friends to figure out our connections. We gave all we had and then some.

The Air Force had shown me the world and given me memories I will forever cherish. But the mission and people we would fight and die for were beginning to fade away. Skills I spent years perfecting no longer mattered in the civilian world. My rank and medals that once brought me instant respect were now just useless artifacts. What happens *after* you spend your life putting service before self? A grateful nation thanks you for your service, but you come home to an empty house and find your "self" left you a long time ago.

The uniform had given me the strength to do the impossible, and while I was wearing it I was unshakable. But after 26 years of serving my country that I loved so much, I knew I was no longer fit for active duty. I had been plagued by depression and was beginning to fear I was losing touch with reality. I tried anti-depressants, counseling, changing my diet, increasing my exercise, working harder, getting regular sleep… nothing seemed to work this time. I had always prided myself on being strong, the one that helped others and never needed help herself, but my confidence was beginning to fade. Would I be one of those veterans who loses their will to live after I left the service? Would it happen right away, or would it be years down the road like my father's generation, fighting with post-traumatic stress for ages before finally succumbing to their wounds?

On my way home from work one night, the grackles, sparrows and mockingbirds gathered in thick dark clouds along the power wires, watching me go into the local grocery store. When I came out at dusk with my roasted chicken and bag of salad, they were thicker, louder… they seemed to be screaming at me to "do something," but I had no idea what it was they wanted me to do. It had been a long day, and the stress was getting to me. I needed to "get my shit in a sock" as Chief T used to say. I walked faster, still in uniform, trying to hold it together so I could get home and feed my family. My old truck wrapped me in safety, the bench seats worn, smelling of dirt and leather. The engine purred and told me when to shift, allowing my tense shoulders to finally relax. Rolling down the window, the soft Texas wind caressed my face and dried my tears as I drove home.

The next morning, I was still thinking about the birds and how I wished I could fly away to see this life from a new perspective. What type of bird would I be if I could fly? At Air War College I had been named the token "dove" in my seminar as we discussed the lessons learned from the Vietnam War.

My classmates were hawks, strategizing what we could have done differently to "win" the war. I fixated instead on the human suffering and the futility of war overall. Nevertheless, I had been a warrior my entire life, and I was pretty good at it. I guess I was a "hawkish dove" not entirely fitting into either camp. Suddenly inspired by the birds, I began to write as if my life depended on it. Something was killing my friends, and I had to stop it before it got me too. I wrote not knowing where the story would take me or what it was I needed to say. Every morning for months, I would wake up before anyone else in the house was awake, settle in on the couch, and peck away on the keys of my laptop.

The characters, which emerged, were important people from my life in their animal form—family, teachers, those I served alongside and against. Coo, a dove raised by hawks, told my story. I wrote about those who cheered me on, and those who made me ashamed to be a woman in a man's world. With tears in my eyes, I wrote about those who killed without remorse, and those who tried to steal my sense of belonging. Inspired, I wrote of the brave Iraqis and the work we did together to rebuild a country torn apart by war. Each chapter brought a lesson I needed to learn or a truth I needed to write. Through writing, I was finally able to feel emotions that had been bottled up for 26 years. As I refined and revised this story, I began to find meaning in my service and purpose for my life after the military.

When I finished the final draft, I felt my *self* return and found the strength to face my biggest challenges yet. This is my story of healing through writing, yoga, and meditation. I am sharing it now to encourage others who are seeking authenticity, peace,

or healing to write and find meaning in their own

words. Each of us is the author of our own stories, I

chose to write mine with a happy ending.

CHAPTER ONE

Coo

Coo's earliest memory was of complete darkness,

yet she was warm and felt the presence of someone

who cared for her. Before she felt the first pains of

hunger, cold, or loneliness, there was peace. Without

sight, she felt no shame of being different. Alone she

had no reason to pretend to be something she was not.

If only she had remained immune to others'

expectations, oh how much suffering she would have been able to avoid. At this moment, she was one with the universe and unknowingly held the secret to save her flock from the dangers to come.

But the day came when peace was replaced by a gnawing hunger deep in her belly. The egg was now too small for her body and she felt as if she would explode if she could not escape. Instincts took over and she began to peck at the shell which once cradled her but now confined her. Softly at first, and then harder and faster as though her life depended on it.

"Dayne!" Maren called with an urgent cry. "Come now, our egg is pipping!"

A large red-tailed hawk circled the scraggly pine and came to rest lightly on a branch just outside the nest. His mouth held a small green lizard, recently dispatched, which he laid gently near his mate. The

two perched with their folded wings touching each
other, watching as a tiny beak slowly pecked a hole
from inside of the egg.

Coo was feeling a new sensation of exhaustion.
Her jaws ached and gravity pulled at her. Just as she
was ready to give up, the shell cracked in half,
spilling her onto her side at the feet of Dayne and
Maren. Her head was heavy and held her to the
bottom of the nest as she greedily gulped the fresh
salty air. Her eyes were mercifully still sealed, yet
even so the bright daylight made her head pound.
Pushing past the pain, she moved her body to explore
her hard-earned freedom.

Dayne gasped, "Oh my, something's wrong with
it! It has no feathers."

Maren nudged him aside as she saw the awkward
pink creature moving toward her. She gently scooped

3

her beak under the fledgling's head, propping it upright against her own breast. "Tear off a tiny piece of meat for our hatchling, dear. She's just worn out and hungry, feathers will come."

Dayne still looked shocked, but did as he was told. He watched as Maren gently fed the creature small bits of meat until it fell into a sound sleep. He knew not to question a mother's love; it was one of the strongest forces in nature. For the next week, Maren never left the nest and Dayne faithfully brought food for her and the new chick. After several days, as Maren had predicted, their chick was covered with soft downy feathers.

On the day her eyes finally opened, Coo was in awe at all the activity below their nest. The soothing whoosh, whoosh sounds she had heard since she hatched were the distant ocean waves crashing on the shore. The raspy voice was the wind tickling clumps of tall grasses crowned with golden tassels of sea oats, like sentries guarding the coastline. Tiny creatures, even smaller than Coo herself, buzzed and hummed all around her. She was entranced, and for a short period of time it felt she was where she was meant to be.

Her parents named her Coo because of the sweet sound she made when they would return to the nest. There was a pleasant routine to her early life. At first light, Maren would depart and bring back tasty seeds and little bugs that tickled her throat as she swallowed them. Her parents would then leave to hunt for the flock as she slept in the afternoon sun, Maren returning periodically to check on her. As the sun set, they would all settle into the nest, talk about the day and tell stories. Life was easy and good.

One day, after her parents left to find more food, Coo accidentally dropped a fat blackberry from the nest. As she longingly looked down at the berry, she saw a tiny mouse creep out of the bushes and approach the fruit. She watched in amusement as the mouse picked up the berry with its delicate hands, and politely took small bites until it was gone; purple juice dripped from its mouth and hands. Completely unaware she was being watched, the mouse licked her fingers clean and then used her hands to wipe the juice from her face and whiskers. Coo made a gleeful sound, startling the mouse, and in an instant, it was gone.

For the next several days, Coo would save a portion of her breakfast; once her parents had left, she would drop it to the ground and await the mouse's return. This continued until the day her father arrived with a tiny lifeless mouse.

To her horror, Dayne placed the dead mouse in front of her and announced, "Coo, it's your big day! It's time for you to start eating like a true hawk."

Coo began to weep.

"What's wrong, Coo?" her mother gently asked.

Before she could answer, her father swooped in and gave her a stern look.

"Why are you crying? Hawks don't cry. Eat your food so you can grow big and strong."

She tried to eat everything they brought, but the meat would often sit in her stomach like a rock. Her father became concerned that she was so pale and small. He would snap at her mother, "See, Maren, this is what happens when you leave an egg unattended for so long. I'll be surprised if she lives long enough to learn how to fly."

Coo hated to hear them argue, so she did her best to grow strong and show them she could thrive and fly despite her apparent shortcomings. Her parents' spats were always about her or the lack of food. She hated to be such a burden. More than anything, she wanted to be like them. Her father was strong and confident; a powerful hunter who could spot movement from miles above the ground. Her mother was graceful and kind. She loved to watch them fly together, riding the thermals and effortlessly gliding past the nest as they scanned the earth and returned with stories of all they had seen.

Her father began to stay away for longer and longer periods. He blamed his absence on the food shortage, which meant he had to fly very far away to ensure the flock had enough to eat. The task of caring

for Coo fell to Maren; it was just fine with Coo

because she adored her mother and could see the toll

her father's wrath was taking on her.

As the days grew warmer, Maren began to stay at

the nest a bit longer to preen Coo's feathers as she ate

breakfast. One morning after she finished eating,

Maren said, "Coo, I think you may be ready for flight

lessons much earlier than the other birds your age.

Although you're small and different from the other

fledglings, you are very agile and fit."

Coo was happy her mother thought she was ready

for flight lessons and she sat up just a bit taller.

"I am concerned your white feathers may be a

distraction for the rest of the flock, so today I'm going

to help you look more like the other birds your age."

Her moment of pride deflated by Maren's comment about her appearance; she turned to see her mother dive to the gully below their nest where the afternoon rains would run off and the ground was made of soft red clay. Coo watched from the edge of the nest as Maren flew down and scooped up some clay in her claws and beak. She flew back to the nest and began painting the distinctive hawk stripes and spots on Coo's head and wings.

"Mom, why're you putting mud on me? It itches and smells funny."

"Well, Coo, I just want you to be able to fit in with all the other fledglings when you start school in a few weeks. Your feathers are different, and some birds don't understand different. You don't want to draw attention to yourself in a bad way. You'll see, this is for your own good."

Coo was silent for a long time as she tried to make sense of what her mother was saying. She was different and it was a bad thing, apparently. Her feathers were coming in soft and white. She didn't have the same flight feathers her parents had, but she knew they worked because when she was alone she would sometimes hop down to a lower branch of their pine tree, and to her surprise, she was able to sort of hop and flap back into the nest. Her beak was also different from her parent's beaks, from what she could see anyway. Is this why her father was gone all the time? Was it because he couldn't bear to look at her? And her mother seemed so sad lately. This was all her fault. She would work hard and try to make them proud when she left for school.

Coo constantly peppered her parents with questions about flying and hunting, begging them to tell stories of all the great hawks they had known.

One night she asked, "Dad, who was the best hawk ever?"

He was silent for what seemed like an eternity. Just as she began to think he would not answer, he spoke. "We are descendants of a hawk named Buteo. He was hatched on an island far, far away, but longed to know more than that small spit of land. His flock warned him that if he left the island, he would surely perish. There was no other land within two days of flight. He was young, strong and fearless. Every day, he would fly just a little farther knowing that someday he would get his chance to leave and see what was waiting for him on the other side of the ocean."

Dayne paused, a distant look in his eyes. Perhaps remembering his own youth and longings to know the world.

"What happened? Is this where he came to? How did he get here?"

Coo's questions brought him back to the present and he continued. "Soon Buteo was capable of flying farther and faster than any hawk the flock had ever known. But his destiny came in a most unexpected way. Late summer brought frequent storms to the islands, some of them strong enough to rip trees up out of the ground and toss them like nest twigs into the sea. Island birds would find shelter in low-lying shrubs and wait out the storm, but not Buteo. He thought it was an opportunity to get stronger and he would intentionally go out and fly against the wind, challenging every storm to best him. Then, one day, a storm took the island by surprise; it was a fast-moving hurricane and, as before, Buteo took to the air instead of finding shelter. He fought through the winds as they overtook the island. Although this storm was smaller, it was much stronger than the others, and he began to tire. Just as he was ready to dive back to earth and find shelter, he arrived in the eye of the storm. It was calm and quiet, but the storm whispered to him 'fly with me.' Buteo stayed there in the eye of the storm and rode it all the way to our shore. He founded a new flock right here and adventurous, strong and brave birds from all around came to join him."

"Wow, that is amazing! Tell me more!"

"This was the place to be. Long before you were hatched, Coo, there were rabbits, mice, giant lizards and all kinds of food in these fields surrounding our nest. Our flock was strong and respected by all for our work in keeping the rodent population in check. But the world is changing and we either need to change with it or perish. When I was your age, we learned to hunt without ever leaving our nesting grounds. Your generation is going to have to leave here and find someplace where hawks can be hawks again."

As he spoke, Coo had an idea of how to help her flock. "Dad, I think I know a way we can help bring some life back to our nesting grounds. When I was younger, I used to drop berries from the nest to attract the mice below. You see they're hungry too, and now that their food sources are going away, they'll move to find food as well. What if you and Mom brought more berries and seeds to plant in the bare earth spots around here? Once they started to grow, maybe the mice would return!"

"Coo, that is a ridiculous idea. We're birds of prey; we don't grow plants. You'll learn our ways soon when you start school. Now go to sleep."

She looked toward her mother, who agreed Coo should go to sleep now, but she winked and nodded approvingly at Coo. Her father may not understand, but she knew her mother thought it was a good idea anyway.

Maren had begun to give her private flying lessons while the rest of the flock was out hunting. By the time she started school she had already been flying longer than the rest of her classmates. As she prepared for her first day of school, her mom repeated the same advice she had given her every day.

"Study hard, little one. You will never be the strongest or the fastest, so you'll need to work harder than all the others. Stay silent and do whatever the other birds do so you don't draw attention to yourself. Always hold your head high and know there is nothing you can't do."

"Yes, Mom. Don't worry. I'll be fine." Although Coo tried to sound calm and confident, her belly swirled like it was full of butterflies. That morning, she had bathed in the mud and eaten blackberries to stain her beak to match the others. Although smaller than the other birds, her mother proudly said she looked just like the other fledglings now.

Maren picked and preened a few of Coo's feathers, nuzzled her beak and then gave her a little push in the direction of the high wires where she would be going for school. Coo flew off with a slight whistle of her wings and landed at the end of a long row of eager young hawks, all ready to earn their place in the flock.

CHAPTER TWO

The Path of Knowledge

The students chattered and nodded at each other

as they began to assemble. It was clear some of them

were nest mates by the proximity in which they

roosted together. Coo kept her distance from them all,

but could feel the cold stares as they tried to figure

out what was different about her. Thankfully, the

arrival of their teachers turned all heads to the wire in

front of them as Screech and Soar landed with a whoosh of their powerful wings. They were an intimidating yet an inspiring pair, and Coo felt a thrill just to be in their presence.

"Good morning, fledglings! I am your leader Screech, and this is my deputy, Soar. She will be your teacher as you learn the ways of our flock and our role in controlling the balance of nature."

As if well-rehearsed, Soar spoke next. "Many of you may be well aware from listening to your elders that our way of life is under attack. Humans are destroying our trees, turning our hunting fields to solid rock, and polluting our air and water. Although our flock size has remained steady, our resources are dwindling."

Screech spoke again, "We're counting on you, our next generation, to find a new nesting ground so we can thrive once again. When your training is complete, one of you will be selected to lead your classmates to a new nesting area and form a new flock. Take your studies seriously, our future depends upon it." After giving the last words, he gave a knowing look to Soar, spread his wings, and the students felt the rush of air across their faces as he departed.

"Fledglings, as Screech explained, I will be teaching you the skills you need to start your own flock once you leave us. Now, let me see what I have to work with."

Soar began a systematic study of each of the students. Eyeing them slowly, she examined each student beginning with the one furthest from Coo. As Soar's gaze would settle on a student, Coo noticed they would freeze, with their chests puffed out and their heads held high. Soar would then take a side-step and visually examine the next student. Everyone, even the fledglings, knew that Soar took her work very seriously and had no time or patience for foolishness. When it was her turn, Coo puffed up and held her head high, but unlike the other students, she maintained eye contact with Soar. At first Coo saw surprise reflected in her teacher's face, perhaps even a bit of indignation that a mere fledgling would look directly in her eyes. Slowly her gaze scanned Coo's body, and when they locked eyes again, Soar looked puzzled or maybe disappointed. Coo would soon become accustomed to such looks. Although she felt shame and embarrassment, she held her head high and steeled her gaze, trying to exude confidence and strength as her mother had taught her.

Soar shook her head, as if to clear her thoughts, and then announced, "I see I have a lot of work to do with you fledglings. Many of you look as if today was your first day out of the nest."

This was the longest day of Coo's short life so far. Although her eyes were glued to her teacher, she imagined she could feel the icy stares from the other students.

"Alright, fledglings. Let's begin with learning the core values of the flock:

1. Duty—Ensure the rodent population stays in check.

2. Courage—A hawk is always ready for the fight and never backs down.

3. Flock First—You must put the needs of the flock above your own.

Our mission is of critical importance. If we do not maintain control of the rodents, they will spread plague and pestilence to the animal kingdom. For each of these values, there are rules which must be memorized and followed. Any bird who chooses not to live by the laws of our flock will be banished."

The fledglings were wide-eyed as Soar began the first of many lessons regarding the rules associated with each of the core values.

"Now that you have left the nest, you will find your own perch where you will maintain vigilant guard. If one of you needs to rest, at least two others will remain alert to defend the flock."

Coo looked around at the other birds. They were her family and yes, she would defend them with her life if that is what was required. As the lessons continued, Soar explained where and how they were to hunt to maintain healthy rodent populations. In the

past, Coo had dreaded eating the food her father

brought in, but she now began to understand the

importance of their mission and felt proud to be

protecting the animal kingdom from suffering. There

was a purpose behind their hunting and compassion in

their methods.

"As hawks you must learn to discern in your

hunts. Hunting sick rodents is off limits; only

scavengers like the vultures can eat the sick without

themselves becoming diseased as well. Also, it is

considered poor form to kill helpless young creatures

not yet able to run, so raiding nests is forbidden."

A large, emboldened student named Jay

interrupted, "But Soar, you and Screech said there's a

shortage of food and that's why we need to find

another home. Clearly there aren't enough rodents to

spread disease here, so why do we need all these rules anyway?"

Soar responded with more patience than Coo thought he deserved, "These *rules* have served us since time began and all creatures were created to live in harmony. It is our duty as hawks to fight against greed, disease and suffering. Our work here is almost finished, and we must find a new home or risk contributing to the destruction occurring around us."

Jay looked away and mumbled only loud enough for his classmates to hear him, "I don't see any humans going hungry down there. Maybe we need to be more like them if we want to survive."

Coo was embarrassed by Jay's arrogant attitude toward their teacher, but he did have a good question. Although Coo understood that the rules were necessary, Soar's response filled her head with even more questions.

As if Soar knew dissension was brewing with the students, she warned, "Those who ignore their worldly duties as hawks not only fail the flock, they fail their true selves and will live a life of woe."

Just as she was beginning to work up the courage to ask a question, the subtle sounds of beating wings drummed in her ears. The flock was returning to the trees after a day of hunting, and dusk was beginning to fall.

"That's enough for today class, go home and rest. I expect you all to be back and ready to learn at dawn tomorrow." The wire shook as Soar launched her powerful frame into the air and disappeared into the trees.

Coo returned to her nest and was relieved to see her Mom had collected a small pile of her favorite foods. She hadn't even realized she was hungry until the first morsel hit the bottom of her stomach.

"How was your day, Coo? Did you make any friends? What did you learn? Did your teachers say anything to you?" Maren asked quickly, as if she could not wait to hear the answers to those questions.

Coo was so hungry she just gave one-word answers as she gobbled her food. "Good, no, a lot, no…" Once her belly was full, she melted into a fitful sleep. Maren settled in next to her, rested her head over Coo's back, and sighed with a mixture of relief and gratitude.

The next day, Coo awoke well before dawn and went down to the gully to camouflage herself in mud. She was one of the first to arrive at the wire and she carefully positioned herself at the far end to keep her

distance from the other students. Coo kept her eyes

trained on the horizon and as the sun appeared so did

Soar, almost as if they had been released from the

same cage.

"Alright, students, I know you have a lot of

questions, but today we're going to take our first

flight together as a flock. I will lead and you will fly

as close as you can to your classmates without

touching." With no further instruction, she launched

into the air and headed toward the sea.

Confusion and panic filled the air as sixteen

fledglings launched to follow. Baby feathers rained

down to earth as they followed Soar on their first

flight together. Slowly, the fat cloud of birds came

together, and Coo felt the exhilaration of flying in a

flock. At first, the draft of wind from the other birds'

wings made her unstable, but as she adjusted the beat

of her wings, she found the flock made her stronger.

Soon it seemed all the fledglings found their pace and

place to enjoy the freedom of flight.

CHAPTER THREE

Flying in Formation

Although Coo enjoyed sitting in the warm sand

where she could close her eyes and let the sound of

the waves soothe her mind, she was driven to work on

her flying skills and would often fly long distances

alone. She had chosen a perch close to her parent's

nest, but she was rarely ever there and only saw her

parents when the flock would gather in the trees at

sunset. She loved them dearly, but knew she would have to be successful for them to love her as much. She imagined how proud they would be if she was chosen to lead the new flock and this fueled her to work even harder.

As dusk approached one evening, she heard hawks screaming and scolding. Scanning the sky and ground for intruders, she prepared herself to defend the flock. When her eyes finally locked on to the movement, she realized it was just another hawk. She blinked a few times in disbelief and cocked her head to the side. It looked like he was carrying a giant pink plastic flamingo in his talons. She had seen these monstrosities before, down where the humans gathered, but never thought she would see one fly. He circled the nesting ground, came to a hover at the tree where she knew Jay perched, and wedged it into the branches in clear sight of the entire flock. He circled around a few more times and then came to rest on a branch near Coo.

"Hi there. My name's Claw. I've seen you in class, but you never stick around afterward to talk to any of us. What's your name?"

Claw was a large bird, but his self-confidence made him seem even larger. Unlike Coo, he was comfortable with who he was, and she admired the way his spirited personality elevated the mood of those who came in contact with him. She was quite surprised, however, that he would make an effort to talk to her.

"Yes! I mean, hello. My name's Coo. Can I ask why you brought that *thing* to our nesting grounds?"

"Oh, that?" Claw asked as he turned his head to look over his shoulder. "That's a gift for Jay. We were sharing a tree, but he would not stop chattering about how we should be more like the humans and abandon our traditions. I decided perhaps I should find a new perch. But being the generous hawk that I am, I left him a little present so he wouldn't miss me. Mind if I take up residence here in your tree? You won't even know I am here." He winked and then hopped from branch to branch testing for a sturdy perch.

He didn't wait for an answer as he began making himself at home. Although she was a bit unnerved at his sudden intrusion, Coo was happy to have the company. Everyone loved Claw for his easy style and good humor, yet he was also a skilled aviator and hunter. Unlike the others who were similarly skilled, Claw seemed to have compassion for others and Coo sensed that he understood her in a way even her own parents could not.

As the weeks of intense training wore on, she found there were very few birds she could call friends. Claw was her first friend and he introduced her to another bird named Lit. Lit was the kindest hawk she had ever met. She would let the others eat first, even when it was her catch, and she was generous with her time and attention. She reminded Coo of her own mother, strong and self-reliant yet always seemingly able to help others in need.

One day, Lit asked her, "Coo, who do you think they'll select to lead the new flock?" Coo thought for a moment and realized that in her mind she had been preparing to lead the flock, even though she knew the odds were not in her favor.

"I'm not sure, Lit, but I trust Screech and Soar to choose wisely. Are you interested in being the leader?"

With more conviction than she had ever shown before, Lit replied, "Definitely not! I've seen the way Jay and his friends try to sabotage anyone who Soar compliments. I'm sure Jay will be selected because he'll try and take out anyone who gets in his way. I'll serve the flock in my own way."

Claw had been eavesdropping on their conversation, and he hopped over to be included. "Well, I think Coo would be an excellent leader. We need someone smart to make sure we find the best home. Jay may have the brawn, but he definitely doesn't have the brains. Also, Coo is different, and our leaders have been telling us we need something different if we're to survive the changes going on around us."

"Thank you, Claw, I think you'd be a wonderful leader as well. Here comes Soar; she's going to announce which one of us will lead our last formation

flight."

Soar stared at the students until the chatter

stopped. Every week, a different student was selected

to lead a formation flight. These flights were an

opportunity to practice their flying skills as a group.

When everyone worked together to match their

speeds and stay in a perfect 'V' shape, they could fly

for hours without getting fatigued. The leader, at the

pointy end of the V, would set the pace and tempo.

Although leading the formation was physically and

mentally challenging, it was a great honor to be

chosen.

"Students, you are all making excellent progress

and have demonstrated you're almost ready to start

your own flock. Today is your final formation flight.

Formation flying is not only about leading, but also

demonstrating that you can follow and support your leader. Coo, we have selected you to lead this final test."

Jay complained vigorously, "She'll slow us all down! She's so small and puny it takes three flaps of her pathetic wings for every one of mine. Why does she get to lead?"

Soar silenced him with an icy stare and most of the students glared at him as well. Soar continued, "I won't be going with you on this flight. We are approaching the day for your solo flights and you need to learn how to get along on your own. Today is an important opportunity for you to think about what our flock needs. When you return, Screech and I will meet with each of you to hear your thoughts on what you think would make an ideal home for the flock.

Soon after that, we will make a decision on which of you should lead the new flock."

Coo swallowed her fear and told herself she would not fail, not today. She had visualized Soar's instructions and knew the area well. Being selected for this honor must mean she was in the running to be the new leader.

Claw swaggered up and said, "You got this, Coo. I'll be flying right here on your wing."

She turned and saw Lit bobbing her head as well.

"Thanks, Claw," she said softly before addressing the others.

"Okay, flock. You heard what Soar said, just follow me and I'll lead us through the pattern and back here. All you have to do is observe areas you think would make the best home for our flock and think about what you will report back to Soar."

She directed each of them to their position in the formation, being sure to keep Jay toward the back. Her nervousness disappeared as soon as they took flight. She bore the brunt of the wind, but knew she was more familiar with this terrain than any of the others. Knowing the flock was counting on her gave her a surge of energy and she felt stronger than she had ever felt before. She found the perfect altitude for observation and her wings beat steady even though she had to work much harder than the others to give them a comfortable speed.

Then, from the back, she heard Jay singing: "Sisters, brothers, have you heard… we gotta follow dirty Coo-Coo bird… She's the weakest of the flock… a flying chicken, bock, bock, bock… when Coo-Coo bird is in the lead… I can't wait till I am freed… When I'm free, you will see… rats and mice,

40

all will flee… For when I fly… they will die… a

smorgasbord for you and I… "

Several of Jay's buddies joined in on another

round, but Coo flew on. Of course, they were singing

in rhythm to their own wing beats. They must have

thought they could slow her down or throw her off

course with distractions. She mentally shut them out

so she could maintain air speed and not fly off course.

How could they sing such vile songs? They had been

taught in school to respect all life. It was beneath

them to enjoy killing when their higher calling was so

honorable. She thought for a moment that Jay and his

friends would break formation and fly off on their

own, but they followed until the entire team returned

to the wires.

After they landed, Coo was angry and hopped

over to Jay. "Your behavior was despicable, Jay!

Were you trying to distract and slow me down? This was an important assignment; don't you care about finding the best nesting ground for our new flock?"

"Settle down, Coo-Coo bird. I already know the best location for our flock, and you didn't even take us near there. I can't believe Soar let a bird like you lead our final formation. You don't belong with us. I'm not sure what you are, but I know you are not a hawk!"

She was just about to ask him what he meant, when Soar called her name.

"Coo, since you were the lead, you will be the first to give your report on where you think our flock should relocate. Follow me; Jay, you are next."

CHAPTER FOUR

The Awakening

Coo's mind was whirling as Soar called her

forward. She quickly made a report but now couldn't

remember what she said. Jay's words still buzzed in

her head… "You are not a hawk…"

As soon as she was dismissed, she flew to the nest

where her mother was sitting on new eggs. Trying to

control the emotions flooding her head, she said,

"Mom, am I a hawk?"

Maren looked shocked at first, and then with a slight quiver in her voice, she asked, "Why're you asking that, Coo?"

"Jay said I'm not a hawk. If I'm not a hawk, what am I?"

"Oh, dear, I knew this day would come. Please come here and sit beside me."

Coo was apprehensive and took only a slight step closer.

Maren looked around as if to make sure no one else could hear, and then she began, "Your father doesn't know this, but our chick from last season died in the shell. When I discovered it was never going to hatch, I pushed the still egg out of the nest and covered it with moss. I was going to tell him when we returned from hunting that night, but he got back

before I did, and I was shocked to see him sitting on

an egg. He was so proud of himself because he had

found a new hunting ground and had returned with a

fat vole. He never even noticed it wasn't our egg, and

I feared telling him. He'd become quite foul-tempered

because of the food shortage and I was still grieving

my loss.

I wasn't in my right mind, but all I could think

about was the desperate situation that would drive a

mother bird to lay an egg in someone else's nest.

Instincts just took over and I decided not to tell

anyone what I knew. When you hatched and wobbled

over to me, nestling in under my wing, I was done in.

The warmth of your tiny pink body next to mine felt

right, and I knew at that moment I was meant to

protect you and raise you as my own. I did my best to

help you fit in, and you really have brought a

wonderful new perspective to all our lives with the

way you study and figure things out. You're always so

peaceful, and we're better for having you in our flock.

Please, don't be angry with me."

Coo was angry, but not at Maren. She could never

be mad at her. However, right now, she did not want

to be here in this nest. She had always thought her

mother was so strong, but now she looked weak and

scared. It was too much for her to bear.

"It's ok, Mom, I'm not mad at you. I just have a

lot to think about. I'll be back once I figure out who I

am."

Coo took flight, and after several hours of aimless

flying, she came back to perch in a lone pine tree on

the outskirts of the flock. So many things, which were

foggy in the past, were coming into focus now. The

mud baths, the distaste for hunting, her size and wingspan. It was quite ridiculous now to think that she belonged here, yet this was the only home she knew. Questions began to flood her mind. Did everyone know she wasn't a hawk? How could it be so obvious to everyone but her?

It was the day before their solos and there were no more classes left, thank goodness. These flights were a rite of passage to mark their status as an adult. As adult hawks, they were able to defend their home and ready to support the mission. On the day of their solos, they would be required to spend the entire day hunting alone and then at sunset return with their prey for the flock's celebration dinner. Some of the students were nervous; it would be their first time flying without the support of the flock, so they were told to go home and spend some time with their families. Coo had no doubts about her ability to perform the final test, but she wanted nothing to do with her family or flock right now.

She looked down from her perch and spotted a nest of baby rabbits, which had been exposed after one of the human machines had cut the tall field grasses where the mother had made her burrow. She recalled Soar explaining how hawks were prohibited from feeding on those too young to live outside the nest. Unsure of when the mother rabbit would be back, or if she had even survived the wrath of the machines, Coo fluttered down to cover the kits with some of the cut grass to keep them warm and safe from predators less civilized than the hawks.

Luckily, the kits were old enough to have a soft coating of down, and although their eyes weren't open yet, they looked like they would be very soon.

Coo spoke softly to them, "Hey there little guys, I know you must be scared. The worst of it is over now, the machines are gone, and I'm going to cover you with this sweet grass. Feel free to nibble your way out of the nest and you'll have an entire meadow to frolic in soon." Coo covered them up and watched as they snuggled next to each other for warmth. She gazed at the nest and fondly remembered her innocence before her eyes had opened.

Suddenly, a voice behind her said, "Whatcha got there, Coo-Coo bird, did you find a big nest of snacks and decide to keep them all to yourself?"

It was Jay and two of his friends. They must have been watching her, and she felt a sick feeling in her stomach. Jay knew that feeding on nestlings was prohibited, but she wouldn't put it past him to try and harm these kits.

"Jay, you know these rabbits are too young to eat. Remember Soar saying 'anyone who chooses not to follow the rules will be banished'?"

"Those ridiculous rules will change when I'm in charge. The world has changed, Coo, and we need to change with it if we want to survive. Now, get out of our way or you will regret it."

Coo spread her wings and covered the nest with her body. She looked up and pleaded, "Jay, please go somewhere else to hunt, these kits have been through enough already."

"Oh, spare me, Coo. You and those kits don't know what suffering is. Life is hard and you need to toughen up if you want to survive. Did you know I had a brother, Coo? That's right, my parents had two hatchlings, but they had to choose one to live and one to die because they didn't have enough to feed us.

They were rule followers like you. I'm sure they regret letting my brother die while these vermin continue to live; that's a decision they're going to have to live with the rest of their lives. Get up off the ground and start acting like a bird, we'll put these vermin out of their misery and be on our way."

Coo closed her eyes and willed herself to stay connected with the earth. She could feel the little rabbits squirming under her weight and their tiny hearts racing. But Jay and his friends were determined to move her. Together they scooped their beaks under her chest, tossing her out of the way to expose the nest below.

She couldn't bear to watch, so she took flight. Rabbits are stoic and silent all their lives until the moment death arrives. Then, they let out a single tragic scream. As she flew away, Coo heard seven tiny death shrieks that drove her away from the only

home she had ever known. The terrible sounds would

haunt her dreams in the months to come.

CHAPTER FIVE

The Storm

Coo flew south, faster than she had ever flown,

fueled by anger, disappointment, frustration and loss.

She had no idea where she was headed, or what she

would do when she got there. She just wanted to be

away. After a bit, the steady beat of her wings and

rhythmic breath calmed her, yet the thoughts of Jay

and her flock remained. How terrible it must have

been for Jay to watch his sibling starve in their nest, but that could not excuse his behavior. He seemed to enjoy being cruel and inspiring rebellion in the flock. She wished she could have been a bee buzzing by while Jay gave his report on what he felt would be best for the new flock. She began talking to herself, "Such an arrogant bird, I certainly hope Screech and Soar can see through his bluff and know he's not the type of leader we need." Then the realization hit her, there was no more 'we' now. She was alone; a bird without a flock.

Just yesterday she wanted to be the one chosen to lead the flock to their new home. The bird she was yesterday, before she learned she wasn't a hawk, was confident and ambitious. She believed she was doing something important. Today she didn't know who she was, where she was going, or what she would do when she got there. She could feel something changing in the air around her, and it filled her with a sense of doom.

The sky began to darken, and the wind picked up. It was almost as if the weather was trying to match her mood. She could see the storm brewing out over the water, and knew she would have to find shelter soon. She thought of the story her father had told her about Buteo and how he took shelter in the eye of the storm and rode it to a new land. At the time, she imagined she was one of those adventurous birds, but now, as it began to sink in that she was not a hawk, she knew she would never survive such a feat.

She found a low-lying clump of trees sheltered on two sides by a human nest. Settling into a perch, she watched as the first sheet of rain arrived.

For what seemed like days, the rain beat the ground. The winds howled and violently tossed anything not firmly attached to the earth. Coo was soaked to the bones but was determined to hold on and survive. The water continued to rise, and the sea threatened to carry her away. When she thought perhaps this was the end for her, the storm stopped, and miraculously the sun began to shine as if nothing had ever happened. The lack of noise and wind filled her with a sense of relief. Her breath was no longer constricted in her breast and she felt her ribs expand taking in the warm moist air. This day was a gift and she was overwhelmed with gratitude.

Unsure of what to do, she did the only thing that felt natural and began to fly. She continued on her course due south, following the coast, trying to distance herself from the flock and her past. The landscape looked different, mangled and broken from the storm.

Hunger began to cramp her belly. She scanned the earth for someplace to stop and eat, but the beach below appeared devoid of life. It appeared the storm had taken a huge bite out of the coastline leaving nothing but bare rock, trash, and sticks. The beautiful sandy beach, and all the creatures who had once lived there, were gone. Disheartened, Coo turned away from the coast and began to travel inland until life reappeared, then flew south once more. Her hunger was replaced by an intense sadness. She mindlessly flew on, trying to make sense of how the life she once knew was changing.

Suddenly, a deafening *boom* shook the air around her. Hit by the invisible wall of sound, she began tumbling toward the ground. As she fell, a wave of frightened birds flew past her shrieking as they rose up from the bushes. She righted herself and came to land in a small tree. Her head was still ringing when she heard a distant *whoop, whoop, whoop* noise. She watched in amazement as two giant metal flying machines approached a swath of the humans' black earth, hovering for a moment and then settling down to the ground. The *whoop, whoop* became a high whine, which slowly faded away. Soon, a smaller machine rolled up and the humans walked toward it and got in. She followed them with her gaze as they drove off to what looked like a colony of human nests, all bustling with activities.

The sun was beginning to set, and she was still stunned by all she had witnessed and the explosion which had knocked her out of the air. Exhausted and confused, she flew toward the ocean in an effort to get away from the humans. She flung herself in the water to wash off the clay that made her skin itch, then sprang back out flapping and snapping the water from her wings. Finding no trees to roost in, she settled into the sand near a clump of tall grasses. She knew the dangers of nesting on the ground but no longer had the energy to care. Intent on resting her eyes for just a few moments, she sank deeper into the sand.

When she opened her eyes, it was morning. The silly seagulls were screaming as they ran up and down the beach trying to catch small crabs and fish. They were so selfish and foolish; snatching food out of each other's beaks instead of working together to collect food for the flock. Their incessant screaming was unnecessary and ridiculous. Coo was hungry and irritated.

She had fallen asleep without eating and was so weak she knew she would have to find something to eat on the ground. Sensing a rodent nearby, she stilled to listen for the soft sound of movement in the seagrasses. When her prey neared, she tensed and pounced feet-first on the soft brown body of her next meal. Without talons, her toes curled around its fat middle as it let out a little squeak of surprise.

The next sound she heard would change her life forever. As she held the mouse in her grip, it spoke to her.

"What the hell are you doing, you stupid bird?"

CHAPTER SIX

Hadi

The shock of his words made her lose her grip,

yet to her surprise, he did not run away.

The mouse held his ground and said, "Why in the

world would you try and eat me? Doves don't eat

mice." Then he picked up a couple of sea oats that

had scattered in their scuffle and said, "Eat these

instead!"

Starving, Coo aggressively ate while the mouse continued to stare and smooth the belly fur ruffled in their scuffle. The oats were soft and satisfying.

After she gobbled the oats, Coo asked, "How did you know I was a dove?"

The mouse gave her an odd look and said, "I know because of your white feathers, your small features, golden beak, and soft feet. There are birds that eat mice like eagles and hawks, those that pick tiny crustaceans out of the sand like sandpipers, and those that eat plants and bugs like you—a dove."

Coo continued to listen since the bold little mouse seemed unusually wise. The mouse said his name was Hadi, and he informed her it was his beach. Hadi told Coo that he came here after the hawks nearly wiped out his entire family.

"Those hawks are out of control and have already decimated one beach. If it weren't for the flying humans protecting us, we'd be in danger here, too. These humans scare away most birds with their thunder-maker because they don't like them near their flying machines. Unlike most humans, these ones understand we're on the verge of extinction and have decided to protect us and the homes we've made here. We finally have a place where we can thrive and tend the sea oats. Someday we hope to restore our original beach and return home."

Coo bristled at his accusations against her flock. Everyone knew the mice were pests and spread disease. However, after realizing how foolish she must have been to believe she was a hawk, she decided to listen for a little longer. Perhaps she had been wrong about a lot of things. She remembered the barren beach on her flight south and considered it

may be the home Hadi was describing.

"I don't understand," said Coo. "What do

mice have to do with sea oats?"

"If it wasn't for us mice, this beach would be a

wasteland like up north," said Hadi. "The beach

where I was born has probably been washed away by

tides after yesterday's storm. My family lived there

until we were hunted so ruthlessly. You birds don't

seem to understand that without mice to harvest and

sprout the sea oats, the sand dunes would cease to

exist. Without the sea oat grasses, you don't have

sand dunes; without dunes, the tides and wind will

steal the sand and our homes with it. As we perish, so

will others, and eventually the hawks too when

they're left with nothing to eat."

As Hadi explained the importance of the beach mice, a strange feeling began to grow in Coo's belly. She thought of what Jay had said about finding another home where none of them had been before. Was it him and his terrible pack of lawless friends that had brought this mouse's family to the point of near extinction?

Back at school, she had been so proud of the organized and efficient plan her flock had put in place to make sure the world was safe; free of disease and plague carried by the rodents. Now doubt began to grow in her mind. If the flock followed Jay's lead, could it result in the terrible future Hadi described? No, that was ridiculous. For her entire life Coo had been taught that rodents were vermin, stupid little creatures that were put on earth for food and had to be controlled so they did not overpopulate. What was she doing listening to this mouse? He was just trying to save his life by making her feel sorry for him.

But still, she was fascinated by this little mouse and how he would pause frequently to just stare at her. Perhaps he was surprised that a bird would listen to him.

"I need to get back to work. If you're interested, bird, you can come with me."

She thought for a moment, then was surprised to hear herself say, "Sure, I've no place else to go."

As the midsummer sun rose and the heat started to build, all creatures began to slow down. Coo followed Hadi and noticed how he had to stop frequently, his tiny chest rapidly heaving to take in a breath.

They paused in the shade, turning their heads to try and capture just a few more moments of the morning breeze. "Normally, we beach mice are nocturnal. I'm not accustomed to being out in this blasted heat. There're so few of us left now, we must work day and night to collect food and care for the mousekins. We're fighting for our lives; humans are paving over our homes, the cats they bring with them are hunting us, and so is every other predator as their food sources dwindle. But we fight to survive because we know that this perfect world that has been gifted to us loses part of its brilliance when any one of its creatures ceases to exist. Once we perish, others won't be far behind."

Coo said nothing in return. She still didn't fully believe his story about the connection between mice and sea oats and wanted to see for herself what they did at the burrows.

Hadi walked to the next spot of shade under a low palmetto plant, and Coo had to duck her head to follow him. She settled down on the sand, and once

he caught his breath he continued, "The sea oats are

our primary source of food, but our burrows also

contain the nutrients needed to germinate and sprout

the oats. Our ancestors understood they needed to

take care of these plants so we'd always have enough

food. We're almost there, you'll see."

They began walking again, Hadi in the lead and

Coo following a short distance behind. She laughed

aloud when she saw the mice running to greet Hadi,

then turning to run in the opposite direction when

they spotted her.

He went to the burrow entrance and called the

mice back out. As they assembled timidly, he said,

"Family, I've brought this bird back to help us. She'll

not harm you, please treat her as part of our family

and get back to work."

The mice gasped and whispered in awe at their leader who had tamed a bird. But how would this bird be able to help them? They began to move in and out of their burrows bringing up sprouted sea oats. Hadi explained they would be taking these sprouts back to the decimated beach in the hopes of someday rebuilding the home they had fled. Each mouse could only carry one sprout at a time, and the journey back to the desolate beach was perilous.

Coo was beginning to feel impatient. Perhaps Jay and his friends did cause this problem. As much as she hated him right now, he was part of her flock and she still carried the promise of "Flock First" in her heart. She may never return there, but she surely didn't want to see them starve.

"Hadi, this is impossible, it'll take all night for a mouse to carry these plants back to that beach. That's if they even make it with all these cats around at night. Let me just fly it there and be done with it."

Hadi examined her carefully and replied, "As you wish, bird."

"You can call me Coo. Now, let's find something to wrap up these plants so I can take them all up to the beach at once."

She flew off to find a bit of material that would work as a makeshift sling. When she returned, the mice had assembled a huge pile of sprouted oats.

Hadi gave her specific instructions on where and how to plant the oats. "Start with the barren beach closest to us and work your way north. Someday my tribe hopes to return to where we came from and we'll need coverage to get there."

Coo took off with the oats and planted them as instructed. As she was resting at the lifeless beach, she recalled the lessons Soar had taught them and

finally understood why the rules of hunting were so

strict. Now that she saw what was at stake, she made

it her new mission to stay until they were able to heal

the damage that had been done. It would take several

weeks, maybe months to bring this wasteland back to

life. Although her flock continued to occupy her

thoughts, she no longer felt she belonged there. She

didn't belong here either, but they needed her, and it

would give her something to do until she could figure

out where to go next.

Coo would spend the mornings flying sprouted

sea oats to the abandoned beach. Hadi taught her how

to tend the plants, which would eventually hold back

the sand dunes and hopefully restore balance.

Each afternoon, the two of them would eat

together and watch the waves hitting the shore. Hadi

introduced Coo to new foods that made her feel

stronger and more at peace with her body. Eventually

Coo began to tell Hadi about her life back home.

"Not all hawks are bad, you know. There is this

one hawk, Claw, I think you'd really like. Everyone

likes him. He always made me forget my troubles,

and his outrageous antics made me laugh. In many

ways, he's the exact opposite of me, but when we're

together everything seemed to balance out perfectly."

"Is that so?"

"Yes, I make him better by helping him study and

take his responsibilities to the flock more seriously.

He makes me better too by encouraging me not to be

so serious and have a little fun now and then."

Hadi didn't say much and Coo began to wonder if

this discussion of Claw reminded Hadi of his mate.

She wondered what had happened to her but dared

not ask. Just then, a young mouse walked up and nudged Hadi's shoulder. He looked at her with obvious affection.

"Coo, this is my daughter Eva, I believe she's come to remind me that it's time for my nap."

Eva nodded respectfully toward Coo, but it was clear by the distance she kept that she did not trust her. She nudged Hadi again; he got up and walked with her back to the burrow.

That night, Coo stayed at the beach until the sun set. She watched the ocean change from blue to red, and finally black. At dusk, the evening creatures began to emerge and scurry about on the beach. She marveled at how quickly life had changed for her, yet how easy it was to adjust to this slower pace.

CHAPTER SEVEN

Purpose or Destiny?

The highlight of Coo's day was always the philosophical discussion with Hadi following their mid-day meal.

"See those doves over there? They seem to be at peace and living the life they were born to live."

Coo felt anger stirring inside her as she responded, "Those doves know nothing of life. They look as if they've never known a day of hardship. I know now that I'm a dove, but I'm not like those birds. They wouldn't survive a day in my flock."

Hadi's eyes twinkled just a bit as he looked at her with a slow, sad smile. "You've been given a different path to follow, and I only encourage you to look within to find where you should go next. You've had experiences they haven't had that will drive and shape your destiny. Those doves never tried to eat a wise old mouse, and they certainly have no interest in hearing advice from one. There is a reason you're here with me now, a reason you've endured what you've endured, and a reason you have loved those you love. But you are a dove, and..."

Coo interrupted, "Stop saying that, Hadi. I've told you I am not like those doves!"

Hadi took a step back and gave her a knowing look. "You are no better and no worse than the doves, go talk to them." With a heavy sigh, he turned and walked back to his den.

Coo watched him amble away and then turned her gaze to the two doves sitting in the tall pine. Why did they make her so angry? Could it be that she had been judging them by the same standards the hawks judged her? It is true doves are not as good as hawks at flying and hunting, but what was their purpose? Curiosity now compelled her, and she took flight to find out what motivated these birds.

Coo flew to a branch near the two doves who sat close to each other. Her approach startled them, and they took off with a sharp whistle of their wings. They had barely cleared the branch before they fluttered back with a soft landing to where they had been perched.

The male of the bonded pair regarded her with curiosity. "Well, hello there, my friend. You look like you've come from a distant flock. My name's Java, and this is Pidge. Whom do we have the pleasure of meeting today?"

Surprised at their warm welcome, Coo said, "My name's Coo. I come from a flock up north. I'm just trying to understand what it is that you doves do all day?"

Pidge and Java began to laugh as if she had said something funny. When they realized she wasn't joking, Pidge said, "Why, Coo? That is the strangest thing to say. What do you mean 'you doves'? You're a dove too, aren't you? What is it that *you* do all day?"

"Actually, I live with the hawks and our mission is to keep us all safe from diseases spread by too many rodents. These last few weeks I've been living with the beach mice and helping them plant sea oats." As soon as the words left her, she felt the shame of an imposter. She tensed her body and started to fly off when Pidge locked eyes with her.

She grounded Coo with her warm gaze. "That is the most interesting thing I've ever heard! Please stay and tell me more. Java here was just going to scout out some potential spots for our new nest, and I'd love to hear all about you." Her dark eyes and soft voice put Coo at ease.

Java rubbed his head on Pidge's neck and said, "All right, I'm out... you chicks have a nice chat." And off he flew.

Pidge walked across the branch and cocked her head to get a better look at Coo. "So, tell me more. Tell me why you do all these things with the hawks and the mice?"

This was not what Coo wanted or expected. She only wanted to find out what the Doves thought their purpose was, but now it would be rude not to respond.

"Well, I was raised by the hawks. Until recently, I thought I was a hawk, just a bad one. They taught me that we all have a job to do in life, and ours was to keep the rodent population from getting out of control. I worked hard to train and learn all about our mission. We all protected each other and fought to keep the world free of disease. But now I see that I'm not a hawk, and I'm trying to repair the damage done by some members of my flock who broke our rules. These mice are on the edge of extinction, and I need to repair the beach by planting more sea oats. That's my purpose now. But I'm curious. What's your purpose in life, Pidge?"

Pidge cocked her head to one side and back again. "Really fascinating story... but I don't understand this *purpose* you are asking me about."

At first, Coo was irritated. What kind of creature doesn't understand its purpose? It was the first thing Coo thought of every morning and what kept her awake at night when she fell short of meeting her own expectations. *What kind of inferior bird doesn't know its purpose?* She took a deep breath and then, as if talking to a hatchling, said, "A purpose is the reason you're here, your inspiration. It's what drives you to do what you do. The hawks keep the world safe from disease by ensuring the rodent population doesn't get out of hand. To do this, they have to sharpen their skills in flying and hunting. So, every day, when I believed I was a hawk, I would train to fly faster, farther, and dive steeper. My purpose is what kept me going when I wanted to quit. I knew that I was part of something much bigger, and that was important to me. All creatures must have a purpose, but I don't understand the purpose of doves."

Pidge continued to cock her head from side to side, trying to understand. "So is the purpose of rodents to spread disease, then? Why would one choose to have a purpose like that?"

Coo felt her irritation growing. Clearly, Pidge wasn't smart enough to understand this simple concept. "You don't choose your purpose! You are born to it. Rodents are food, their purpose is to be hunted." As soon as the words left her throat, she regretted it.

Coo noticed a bit of alarm in Pidge's eyes as she said, "But Coo, I thought you said the beach mice maintained the sea oats? What kind of inspiration is it for them to exist only to be food for another animal?"

Pidge's simple logic made Coo feel like a raving idiot. "I'm sorry; I know I must sound crazy. I suppose I'm just trying to figure it out as well. I've never thought of anyone's purpose other than my own until these last few weeks. Now I'm uncertain what my own purpose is if it's not to be a hawk."

"It's alright. I see you're troubled by this, and I want to help. I don't suppose I've ever thought of my life's purpose before, and I'd be foolish to assume all doves have the same purpose. The hawk's purpose, although noble, doesn't sound at all appealing to me. Java and I eat seeds when we're hungry, splash in the water when we're hot, and we like searching for nice trees where we can build a nest and maybe raise

chicks someday. I suppose our purpose is to be kind

to each other. That's enough for me. We're at peace,

and don't feel the need to change anything or

anyone."

"But, Pidge, isn't there something more? A goal, a

dream, a hope for something that's hard to attain?

Something to devote your life's work toward?"

"I am sorry, Coo. I really don't understand how

wanting something that I have to sacrifice and work

for will make me any happier or more fulfilled than I

am now. I'm happy with life as it is, and at peace with

all I've been given. If I wanted for more than what

each day brings me, I'd be trapped in perpetual

wanting. And what if I should die before I fulfill my

purpose? Imagine how tragic that would be to have

worked all my life to attain something and then fall

short. It seems to me a purpose will only leave you

wanting more. Life comes with challenges and joys.

I've found I don't need to chase it for the new day to

arrive. I just meet each day with a happy heart and try

to do my best."

Pidge spoke with sincere honesty. Although it

could have been the time of day, it almost seemed as

if she was illuminated from within. Pure light and

kindness shone from her when she spoke. These

doves represented everything she had been trying to

change about herself, but after talking to them, it was

hard to hate them. Her head felt like it was going to

explode as she wrestled with this strange mixture of

emotions. For as long as she could remember, she had

been driven to fly, hunt, and fight for her flock. She

had never stopped to question why, or if, there was

any way of life other than the one she had been given.

Java returned to the branch on which they were perched and snapped Coo out of her deep thoughts. "Pidge, I've found a beautiful tree and I want to show you now before the sun begins to set."

"It isn't near the flying humans' field, is it?" asked Coo.

"No, no… it's too loud there for us. The tree I found is nice and quiet. It's further north, up near the abandoned beach."

"Smart choice," said Coo. They said their farewells and Coo thanked them for their kindness. They had given her a lot to think about.

She looked down and saw Hadi emerging from his den, yawning and scratching. There was something special about this mouse. Her friendship with him was unexpected and she had come to respect his insights. When he first asked her why she felt such dislike for the doves, the image of how she had been

mocked and scorned by Jay for her timid ways and

lack of talent came to mind. She now realized it was

not the doves she was angry at, but herself for not

being a hawk or dove. The doves were so comfortable

with each other and who they were. What she saw in

them was everything she wished she had with her

own flock.

As she flew down to meet with Hadi, she was

hopeful he could provide the clarity she so

desperately wanted. She landed ever so lightly in the

sand next to him and, for what seemed like an

eternity, neither of them spoke.

Finally, Coo said, "I'm still not certain who I am

and what my purpose is. The doves seem happy to be

without a purpose, they say they just 'are' and that's

enough. If I'm not a hawk, and I'm not a dove, what am I and why am I here?"

"Only you can answer that question, Coo."

Of course, he would say that, Coo thought in frustration. She was certain he knew the answer, but he was going to make her figure it out. After another long silence, Hadi spoke again.

"You must look within and find your own way. Yours is neither more nor less important than mine or the doves', but it is certainly different. I know it's a lot for you to think about, but you've been out of touch with your body and your mind for quite a while now. You've been more interested in becoming who you thought others wanted you to be than understanding who you were *meant* to be. You learned an important lesson with the doves today."

The seagulls had returned and were flapping and squawking over something that had just washed up on the beach. Coo absently gazed toward the gulls.

"When I believed I was a hawk, I had a purpose in life. Now I feel more like those stupid seagulls, living for the next dead fish to wash up on the shore."

Hadi looked annoyed with her and with an unusual sharpness in his voice said, "What is it with you and the gulls? Perhaps you need to spend some time with them as well. And why do you think you need to be like the hawks to do something great?"

Coo stared at Hadi, not sure if those were rhetorical questions or not.

"This summer you helped rebuild a shoreline destroyed by an imbalance in nature caused by these great hawks of yours. You did that on your own by listening to a little old mouse. I would say you did

something to make the world a better place."

Coo was caught off guard once again. How was it

this mouse could say something so profound that

would make her rethink everything she had known up

to this point?

"What would your life have to look like in order

for you to feel whole, vital, and happy? What do you

need to let go of to become who you were meant to

be? Think about it, and we'll talk more tomorrow."

As Hadi walked back to his burrow, Coo was left

with a strange sense of power she had never felt

before. Could it be that she had the power to create a

life where she felt she belonged? Up to this point, she

had only focused on trying to be what others expected

of her, yet here on this beach, she felt a freedom she

never knew existed. The energy of possibilities was

so great that she felt the need to spread her wings and fly. She launched into the air, and flew great circles above the beach, diving, swooping, and even cooing as joy overwhelmed her.

As she fluttered back down to the soft and warm sand, she tried to picture a world where she felt whole. For so long she had focused only on what she needed to do to be more like the hawks. Although it was liberating to think that she could escape their expectations and follow a different road, it was daunting to figure out what exactly that life would look like. She closed her eyes and listened to the hypnotic sound of the waves. She was suddenly taken back to her earliest days in the nest when she was warm and safe. She realized the last time she had felt this peace was before her eyes were opened.

Now her eyes were fully opened in a new sense. If she wasn't meant to be a hawk, then all those things she had been trying to improve about herself no longer mattered. In fact, she didn't care about hunting and soaring. She respected the hawks for their skills, but perhaps she had different ones that were equally important. She sat quietly and searched within for what was important to her now that her vision had cleared.

Love, that was important to her. She loved her family and flock. There were several hawks she admired, and she still felt duty-bound to protect and support them. These last few months she wondered if she would ever return to the flock, but without them, she knew she would never be whole again.

Balance was also important to her. She loved how everything in nature is connected and interdependent in some way. The change of seasons brought an

opportunity for every living thing to flourish in its

own time. The balance between the sun and moon

catered to the needs of every variety of creature. This

disruption of balance as a result of the near extinction

of the beach mice was troubling her as well. She felt a

calling to protect those who were unable to defend

themselves and to teach others about maintaining

balance.

Gradually, she envisioned creating a home where

she could live in safety with those she loved.

Everyone at peace with who they are and celebrated

for their individuality. A flock where each bird is free

to explore and share ideas. Every creature encouraged

to make a positive difference in the world. Yes, if she

had a home like this, she would be a very happy bird.

Yet, there was something else Hadi had asked her to think about once she could envision what it would look like if she felt whole, vital, and happy. She recalled his words. *What is preventing me from achieving it, and what do I need to let go of to become who I was meant to be?*

CHAPTER EIGHT

Letting Go

The next morning, Coo awoke before dawn and

flew to the beach she had helped reseed. The thought

of creating a new life was exciting, but what was it

she would have to let go of before she could become

who she was meant to be? As she distractedly tended

to the oats, she heard the seagulls screaming down on

the beach, and remembered Hadi's recommendation

that she explore her feelings for the gulls. Perhaps they held the answer she was seeking.

She flew over to the shoreline where the gulls were picking apart a dead fish. While one or two would peck at the fish, another would swoop in, announcing their need was greater, and bully their way in to grab a bite. Although there was much complaining, all the birds seemed to be getting what they needed. Their screams were irritating, but she began to admire their tenacity in announcing what it was they wanted and why.

Suddenly, she realized the irritation she felt was not with the gulls, but the life she had lived with the hawks. She had taken the commandment of "Flock First" to the extreme, and denied herself the time she needed to nourish her soul and take care of her body. She began to berate herself. *I ate food I didn't like. I was afraid to speak up for what I believed in, and I*

bathed myself in clay to prevent others from seeing

who I truly was. What kind of life is that! This must be

what I need to let go of to become who I am truly

meant to be!

She couldn't wait to get back and tell Hadi she

had figured it out! She arrived just as Hadi was

creeping out of his den and almost pounced on him.

"Hadi, I figured out who I'm meant to be and

what I need to let go of, and why the gulls irritated

me so…"

"Good morning, Coo, it's nice to see you so early

this morning."

The irony in his voice caught her attention and

Coo suddenly realized how disrespectful she must

have seemed. "Oh, I am sorry. Good morning Hadi."

She waited for him to make a couple of circles and then settle into his favorite spot in the worn grass just outside the burrow. "It's just that I can finally see clearly where I want to go, and who I want to become! I sacrificed who I was, and my sacrifices went unnoticed and unappreciated. The hawks are my family, and my home will always be with them, but that does not mean I have to pretend to be a hawk. Pidge and Java made me see there is nothing wrong with being a dove; in fact, they're remarkable birds. The seagulls are also honorable in their own right; fighting to keep the beaches clean and always speaking their mind. They've shown me it's time I find my voice and return to my flock."

"Well done, Coo. By seeking to become what you were not, you almost destroyed your potential to become something much greater. Although you've accepted yourself and the hawks for who they are be

wary. When you feel the pull back to your old ways,

remember we are all connected. The best part of you

is what unites you with the best part of them. The

things that make you angry at others are merely

reflections of yourself that you have yet to

recognize."

Coo was delighted by Hadi's approval although

she didn't quite understand everything he was saying.

She noted a hint of sadness in his voice as he said,

"You're getting closer, Coo, you'll soon find what

you have been searching for and it will be time for

you to go."

That evening, Coo let the ocean sounds soothe her

as she continued to let go of the anger she had been

holding toward the doves and gulls. Waves washed up

to shore and swept the resentment she had been

holding toward her own flock out to sea. The sun

began to set, and she felt more connected to the world

than she had ever felt before.

CHAPTER NINE

Return to The Flock

As the sky began to brighten, Coo realized she

had spent the entire night planning her next move.

She knew what needed to happen and she waited for

Hadi to awaken.

Hadi walked out of his den, stopped, and held

Coo's gaze for what seemed like an eternity. Finally,

he said, "I see you are ready to go now."

"Yes, Hadi, it's time for me to leave. You've helped me see what I need to do next, and I can never repay you for the lessons you've taught me. I could understand if you said no, but I'd like for you to come with me to enlighten my flock on the dangers of overhunting and destroying the balance of nature."

Coo knew that Hadi anticipated her leaving today and understood she did not yet have the confidence to go alone. Not sure what she would do if he said no, she held her breath until he replied.

"I have already said goodbye to my family, Coo, let's do it."

Coo gently wrapped Hadi in the piece of cloth she had used to carry sprouted sea oats, scooped the ends up in her beak, and together they began the long journey back to her flock. It took several hours, and the precious bundle she was carrying strained Coo's neck and fatigued her wings. Hadi was surely

uncomfortable as well, and although neither

complained, Coo stopped just short of arriving home

to rest and check on Hadi.

They landed between two large dunes along the

familiar coast, richly adorned with sea oats Coo had

flown over hundreds of times without ever seeing.

"How are you doing, my friend?" she asked as Hadi

stiffly walked off the carrying cloth.

"Never better, Coo, never better." Hadi

uncharacteristically launched into a lecture about the

nature of suffering, but Coo was too lost in her own

thoughts of what it would be like to see her flock

again. She listened out of politeness, but the meaning

did not sink in.

Coo was anxious to get back in the air, so as soon

as he finished talking, she began to adjust the carrying

cloth indicating to Hadi that it was time to go. He agreeably took his spot on the blanket, Coo gathered up the ends, and they departed for the final leg of their flight. When they finally arrived, the first bird she looked for was Claw. Spotting him in the tree they once shared, she took Hadi there for introductions.

"Coo, where've you been? We all thought you were dead! I missed you, and so much has happened here at home. Jay's been named to lead the new flock and the ceremony is tonight. And, whoa… why're you carrying a mouse in a blanket?"

Coo and Hadi laughed in unison at Claw's exuberance.

"Well, Coo, I now know what you see in him," Hadi said as he extricated himself from the blanket, stood up on his hind legs, and smoothed his fur. "Claw, they call me Hadi. Coo asked me to come here to address your flock. Together we intend to educate

them on the dangers of overhunting."

Claw dramatically swooned and fell out of the

nest, caught himself mid-air, and flew back up to

where they both sat. "Well, you never do anything

halfway, do you, Coo? Why don't you two tell me

what you have in mind?"

Coo and Hadi began to explain what had

transpired over the summer. They talked of how they

envisioned convincing the rest of the flock that

moderation was required and how each creature had a

responsibility for maintaining the health of the

environment. Claw listened intently and when they

were done, he promised his support, even though he

doubted the message would be well received.

That evening, the flock began to gather in the

trees to witness the ceremony announcing Jay would

lead the new flock. Claw approached the platform set up for the ceremony. In a booming voice, he announced, "Listen up, birds, Coo's returned from her travels and she's brought a visitor."

The usual chatter ceased as all heads rotated toward Coo and Hadi. Coo scanned the flock, looking for her parents. She saw them perched together in a low tree, and at first, her mother's head was down and her wings hung low in defeat. Her father began to shift from foot to foot, obviously uncomfortable. He had never seen his daughter without her camouflage of mud. His movements caused Maren to look toward the platform. When she saw Coo, she immediately brightened. As Coo and Maren made eye contact, a flood of emotions washed over her and Coo felt the love that the two had always shared.

Several birds flew down to join them, and Coo began to explain where she had been and why Hadi was with her. Suddenly, a dark shadow swept over them and Jay landed beside her, pinning Hadi to the ground.

Hadi and Jay locked eyes. As usual, Hadi's gaze was steady and measured, but as Jay turned to look at Coo, she was surprised to see something that looked like fear in his eyes.

As birds began to scatter, Jay screeched, "How dare you take the stage here on the day of my ceremony! You abandoned your responsibilities and now you return with an old diseased beach mouse, demanding attention just like before. You are clearly not one of us, go back to wherever you have been. You're not welcome here in my flock!"

Coo felt heat creeping up from her chest and pressure building in her head. She silently scolded herself; *What had she done! Why did she ever think she could make a difference?*

Just then, Screech and Soar arrived. Screech put his head down, ramming it into Jay's chest and knocking him off of Hadi.

"Hold on there, Jay, this is *not* your flock. When the time comes you *may* have your own flock to lead, but you will never talk to a member of my flock like that again. We want to hear where Coo has been, and what she has to tell us. Lit, take this mouse and get him some water. Coo, start talking."

She took a deep breath and began once more to tell the story of Hadi's beach and how the mice were integral to the sea oats and the environment. With conviction, she told the flock how she had witnessed the devastation due to overhunting, and how they had

worked all summer to repair the damage.

"You see, everything's connected, and every

creature has a unique destiny to fulfill. I believe mine

is to share with you what I've seen so you know what

could happen if the beach mice are not protected."

As she spoke, she could feel the eyes of the flock

on her. Maren was beaming with pride. Dayne looked

as though he wanted to be anywhere but there. Behind

Screech, she could see Jay rolling his head and

sighing as if her words tortured him. When she finally

finished, there was complete silence.

Claw was the first to speak, "I don't know about

the rest of you, but after that speech, I think we

should all go get a drink and chill out for a bit."

Laughter erupted from the flock, along with a few

harsh words from Jay.

Screech silenced them with a look and said, "Coo, you have given us all something to think about tonight. Although I'm sure Claw was joking, I do think it's wise to hold off on the ceremony until tomorrow. There's been quite enough excitement for one evening."

"Thank you for listening, Screech. I'll go collect Hadi and if you want, we'll leave in the morning." Coo flew off to find Lit and Hadi, and Claw followed.

Once safely back at Claw's nest, Coo made sure Hadi was comfortable and fed, then collapsed from exhaustion and fell into sleep.

Claw and Hadi talked, laughed, and drank to life, love, good friends, food, and how eventually all the idiots like Jay will get exactly what they deserve. One by one, the birds who were inspired by Coo's speech stopped by to meet Hadi and tell him how brave it was for him and Coo to bring the news back to the

flock.

In the morning, Coo was the first to rise, but Hadi

was gone.

CHAPTER TEN

Hate vs Hope

In a panic, Coo shook Claw and asked him where

Hadi had gone. Claw was slow to wake and could

only smile and wink at her.

Unable to get answers from Claw, she flew to

Lit's perch and breathlessly asked her if she had seen

Hadi, "Oh, Coo, the last time I saw him was when I

stopped by Claw's nest to check on you. You were

sound asleep, and Hadi and Claw were telling stories. Lots of birds stopped by to meet Hadi and check to make sure you were alright. We missed you, Coo, and we were so worried."

The alarm calls of the flock interrupted their conversation, signaling Soar was calling the flock to gather. High-pitched screeches grew louder every second as each hawk echoed the call. Coo wasn't sure if it was the urgency in the call that made her heart race, or the fact that she couldn't find Hadi.

"I have something I have to do, Lit! Save me a spot next to you at the gathering."

She flew past the training grounds scanning the earth for any signs of movement. Her heart raced and her stomach clench into knots as her desperation to find Hadi grew. Even though she knew every tree and ravine in this area, she still felt like an imposter and

an outsider. Her search for Hadi was futile. Defeated
and ashamed, Coo landed next to Lit to hear why they
had been called to meet. Claw swooped in, pushing
into the small space between Coo and Lit, knocking
them both off balance.

Soar flapped her wings for silence and began,
"Flock, as you know Screech and I announced Jay
would lead the new expedition flock last night prior to
Coo's dramatic return. Nothing has changed with
regard to our decision, Jay will still be leading the
new flock as planned. The ceremony will take place
this evening as the sun sets. Coo, we expect you to
remain as part of the flock and continue your duties.
That is all."

Although deeply disappointed, she knew her
efforts had no impact on Screech or Soar. After

yesterday's events, she was not at all surprised by the announcements.

"Claw, Lit, we need to find Hadi. I'm afraid something terrible has happened to him. I feel awful, this is all my fault. How could I be so foolish to bring him here?"

Claw was beginning to wake up, "I don't understand, he was there with me last night and was a right jolly fellow. We had a few drinks, and everyone was coming by to thank him and say that they respected his courage for coming to deliver such an important message with you. The flock did listen to you, and many of them agree that we shouldn't hunt to the point of annihilation in any one area. Of course, there are those like Jay and his band of goons who are incapable of accepting any new ideas."

"That's it, Claw! Jay must have taken him. He's so full of hate; he would do anything to hurt me. I have to go and see him."

Coo took off toward Jay's nest. Lit and Claw sighed and took off after her.

Coo had become a very fast flyer and arrived well before the others. When she landed at Jay's nest, he was sharpening his talons with his beak. "What do you want, Coo-Coo bird? I'm busy."

"I want to know what you did with Hadi, you evil bird."

Jay feigned surprise. "I have no idea what you're talking about. I saw your stupid mouse friend scurrying south late last night. He must have known he was going to get eaten if he stayed. You really are a crazy bird. Why don't you go back to wherever it is you came from? We were better off without you and let's not even mention that nonsense you spouted to

cause doubt and confusion. This flock needs

leadership and strength, *you* are a threat to our

survival."

Coo lunged at him. Familiar feelings of anger and

disappointment came back in a torrential flood. She

wanted to hurt him the way he had hurt her. They

collided with claws and beaks searching for weak

spots, but he was much stronger than her and she felt

his talons pierce her wings. The pain was

excruciating, but it began to focus her thoughts, and

she recalled Hadi's words about how they were all

connected by the best parts of each of them. He

would be disappointed to see her fighting with Jay, a

desperate act she knew now was based on fear, not

courage. Suddenly, Claw and Lit were there, prying

the two of them apart and dragging Jay to the edge of

the nest. Bloodied and disappointed in herself, Coo

fought the pain in her wings and headed toward the

ocean.

The water called to her and she did not hesitate to

plunge head-first into the deep water. Saltwater stung

her wounds, and she could feel the pulse pounding in

her wings. The steady beat reminded her she was still

alive and still had the capacity to make a difference.

She let the tide pull her toward the shore before

gathering her strength to push off the water and fly

toward a scrubby pine where she would be well

hidden. With an odd detachment, she noticed how her

wings had been colored pink by her own blood.

Closing her eyes, she listened to the ocean and then

listened to herself.

Once her feathers had dried, she began flying

south, hugging the ground as she searched for Hadi.

Soon, she found herself gliding over the newly seeded beach she had spent all summer working on. Flying close to the ground, she could see that life had begun to return to the beach with the smallest of insects, lizards, and birds, and hopefully, soon there would be beach mice again. But no signs of Hadi.

She flew on and saw the tree Pidge and Java had described in such detail during one of their visits. It was a weepy-looking Australian pine tree overlooking a sheltered cove. She stopped and was greeted warmly by her old friends. Three eggs graced the nest and the doves beamed with pride.

Pidge bubbled, "Oh, Coo, thank you so much for all you did to replant the sea oats on this beach. Every day we see this beach coming back to life, and we tell all our friends that *we* know the bird who made it happen!"

"Where are you off to now, Coo? You look like you're in a hurry." asked Java.

Not wanting to bring bad news to their nest, Coo replied, "Oh, I'm headed back to visit Hadi. I'll return to visit after your eggs hatch. I'm sure you two will have some lovely chicks. Congratulations on your new home and growing family." She said the last part with sincerity as she bumped chests with the two doves.

They nodded farewell and she flew on toward Hadi's den. There was a long trail of sea oat grasses now leading to the beach where she had spent many days with her furry little friend. It was a crisp autumn morning, and she recalled Hadi saying how it was his favorite season. He had struggled in the summer heat this year and was looking forward to cooler nights and fresh breezes in the morning. On one particularly muggy summer morning, he told her, "Soon autumn

will be here, and we'll savor the fruits of our labor.

Everything has a season; I rejoice in the new life in

the spring and growth in the summer, but I love fall

the most when I can just pause and breathe deep

before winter puts everything to sleep again."

She landed outside his den. When he did not

appear after several minutes, she knew he was gone.

She sought comfort in remembering all the

discussions she had with him, how he had led her to

understand her emotions and who she truly was. With

his guidance, she had learned to love herself and

equally love all other creatures. Here, she had felt as

if the whole world was her home. Just like the sea

oats, she too had grown over the summer. How was it

that one day back in the flock had caused her to

totally lose those lessons learned, and act like such a

fool? She wished she could find the compassion for others that Hadi had shown her.

From the corner of her eye, Coo caught a slight movement. She continued to stare at the ocean as Eva crept up to sit beside her. Unable to look at her, Coo softly said, "Your father is gone. It's my fault, and I am so sorry for what I've done."

With a gentle, clear voice Eva began, "Coo, my father and I said our final farewells yesterday. He knew he would not be returning, but he felt his journey with you was more important than anything he could have done here."

This was not what Coo had expected. She turned her head to look at Eva.

"Before you arrived, my father was in a very dark place. The hawks had eaten our family and destroyed the beach where he had lived his entire life. He was filled with hatred for them and guilt for not having

been able to stop it. But he was strong and continued

to fight to move those of us who had survived to

safety. In the days before you arrived, however, he

was beginning to tire. We had new predators here, not

much shelter, and we were all just fighting to survive.

It wasn't until you tried to eat him that something

sparked and made him realize he was not done living

yet. You brought light in our darkest hour. When you

took the time to listen and learn about our struggle,

you gave my father the best gift ever: hope. He was

almost young again, and ready to rebuild our lives.

We all began to see the hawks through your eyes, and

understand they were merely fulfilling their duty to

their true selves and doing what they are meant to do.

They're hunters, and I know we're only food to them.

But thanks to you, my hawkish-dove friend, I too see hope for a better world."

Coo had no words. These mice had connected her to the rest of the world and expanded her heart to experience emotion much deeper than anything she had ever felt before. It was an exquisite pain, one that captured the beauty of creation, growth, and the inevitable cycle of decline, death, and rebirth.

Eva went back inside and brought Coo a leaf piled with seeds before returning to her work.

As her mind worked furiously to figure out what to do next, Hadi was with her again, coaching her to respond with wisdom, and not react impulsively to the situation she found herself in. She knew he was no longer alive, but his lessons would always be with her. She was no longer afraid of what others thought or how they would respond. She would do what was right and perhaps others would follow.

She ate the seeds, said her farewells, and thanked Eva before launching toward the north once again. Hadi was on her mind as she flew past the dunes they sought to heal, admiring the beauty and movement of the green grasses against the white sand. The strength and lightness she felt could only be attributed to the weight she had borne by once having carried him. She stopped at the same spot where they rested just yesterday, and she struggled to recall his final teachings. At the time, she had been consumed by thoughts of the future and the impact her return would have. Her desires and impatience overshadowed the wisdom Hadi was offering to her that day. But now she could finally hear his words.

"At our core is pure *joy* but also its opposite *suffering*. Both are available to you at any time, regardless of your circumstances. Remember this is your choice. Your purpose may call you to alleviate the suffering of others, but don't be fooled into thinking this is what brings you joy. If you're waiting for others to give you what only you can summon you will find disappointment."

Remembering these words, she recognized she still had so much to learn. It was true she had expected some special recognition from her flock when she brought Hadi home. It took Hadi, a beach mouse, to show her the wisdom and the true meaning behind the hawk's guiding principle of "Flock First." The flock never asked her to put her needs aside and be a martyr as she had once mistakenly thought; this was her own doing in trying to be better than others.

Buteo and the elders who established "Flock First" as one of their rules to live by were merely trying to teach the highest form of love in this world; service to others when there is no personal gain. Hadi tried to show her this as well, but she had to learn the hard way. As the tides retreated and dusk began to approach, she took flight once again, this time with no expectations, but with a clear purpose in mind.

CHAPTER ELEVEN

A New Beginning

That evening, the flock began to assemble once

again. Jay had arrived early and was puffed up and

strutting back and forth across the platform. He was

impatient for Screech and Soar to arrive and bestow

upon him the title he felt he had earned. He was lost

in thoughts of how he would run things once he was

in charge. His first order of business would be to get

rid of the weak, like Coo, who was always creating such turmoil and distracting the flock from their work.

As is tradition, formal ceremonies always take place at sunset. The chatter of the birds increased in pitch and intensity as the sun began to sink behind the trees. Jay took his place, and the birds became silent as Screech and Soar flew in perfect formation over the trees, then into a steep dive toward the platform. As they flanked Jay, the flock silenced, and Screech began his speech.

"Proud warriors, we share a rich heritage of duty, courage, and family here along this coast. Although our numbers have remained relatively steady, our home can no longer support all of us. After consulting with our elders last winter, we made the decision to encourage a group of young hawks to find a new home where they can grow and prosper. We will miss

our sons and daughters, but we need to give them a

chance at a better life than we have had. It was a hard

decision to pick just one young hawk to lead this

expedition, but Jay has proven he has the courage and

strength to forge a new home for this new flock. Jay,

we are trusting you to continue our traditions and care

for the birds under your care as we have cared for

you. With my authority, I now bestow upon you the

official title of Leader of the Young Flock."

Then it was Jay's turn to speak. "Thank you,

Screech. You have done a fine job leading our flock.

But, my fellow hawks, the time has come for a

change. For years now our leadership has protected

themselves and their traditions, but the birds of this

flock have suffered. The leadership's victories have

not been your victories. The division inspired by

weak birds like Coo and the other bleeding-heart birds has caused strong birds like us to go to sleep hungry at night, while rodents are allowed to roam free and overpopulate our lands. This injustice stops right here, right now. From this day forward, the strong will prevail!"

The flock erupted in chatter, and at first Jay's chest swelled as he clearly thought they were cheering his words. But all the birds were gazing upward at Coo, glowing a brilliant white with the setting sun shining off her back as she approached the platform. This time she did not land but held a perfect, almost silent hover above the stage.

"My dear friends, I have returned tonight to give you an alternative to the flock Jay plans to lead. You have been and will always be my family. However, since leaving here, I've learned the flock I serve is more expansive. I'm not a hawk, yet I admire your

noble way of life. I'm not a dove, yet the doves have

shown me the power of love. Like many of you, I

used to believe we had to control the rodent

population in order to maintain the balance of nature.

This summer, a rodent named Hadi showed me that

no one creature is superior to another, and nature is

not ours to control but to honor. We will rise above

suffering to reveal joy in finding our true selves and

living the life we are called to live. Tonight I start a

new life in a place where all creatures are encouraged

to look within to discover who they are and what they

are called to do. We will respect life and live with

gratitude for all we have been given, taking what we

need and nothing more. If there are any birds who

wish to join me, I'll be flying south to Hadi Beach."

Jay shook his head in disgust and motioned for the ceremony to resume.

As Coo turned to fly away, the air filled with sounds of beating wings. With a heart filled with joy, and the sun setting behind them, Coo led her flock in search of a new beginning. As they passed over the trees where Coo had taken shelter from the storm, she knew there would be more storms ahead, but she no longer feared them. They were a part of her and she was a part of them; she had known all along.

AFTERWORD

Lessons From My Father

The first call came on a hot, sticky summer night in Texas. Claw and I were preparing dinner when the phone rang. The voice was unrecognizable, but caller ID revealed Dayne's phone number.

"Maren is missing, and I'm worried. She was with me this afternoon when we laid down to take a nap. When I woke up, she was gone. Now it's getting dark outside and there's a storm coming. I have to find her. Is she there with you?"

A little more harshly than necessary, I blurted out, "Dad, Mom died five years ago."

With uncharacteristic emotion, he shouted, "No! She was here today. She must be stuck somewhere in the rain, I'm so worried about her. Can you fix it?"

It sounded like his mouth was full of cotton balls. He had been increasingly confused and emotionally volatile these last few months, but this time something was different. Compassion gripped me by the shoulders and shook me awake. I had no idea how to "fix it," but I had to do something.

"It's okay, Dad, Mom is safe, and we'll take care of everything."

That night, he called and hung up at least a dozen times. He was clearly in distress. I called the nurse on duty and she informed me that he'd already been

checked out, his vital signs were fine, and there was

nothing else they could do. Covid-19 was rampant

throughout the country, but the highest rates were in

Florida. By order of the Governor, assisted living

facilities were not allowing friends or family to visit

residents. It had been five months since any of us had

seen him, and his ability to use the phone seemed to

be diminishing.

I had never been particularly close to my father;

memories of him from childhood mostly held

disappointment, fear and sadness. He was a harsh

disciplinarian and had no time for childish behaviors.

When he was not on a remote assignment to Turkey,

Korea or Vietnam, he would leave before we awoke,

return for a silent dinner while watching the news,

and then head back to work again. When I was

younger I always wished he would be there for my birthday, but he never was. As I got older, I no longer cared. He had given the best parts of himself to the Air Force and had nothing left for his family. He tried to make up for the lost years by doting on his grandchildren, but my wounds of abandonment and fear from childhood prevented me from getting close to him as an adult. Yet, if Maren was still alive she would want me to do something. She had such a big heart and boundless compassion for any person or animal who was suffering.

I turned to Claw for strength; my best friend, wingman and husband wrapped me in his powerful arms. After I ranted and raved about everything that was wrong with the world, he simply said, "You need to go get him."

I left the next morning and the chaos which
ensued upon my arrival in Florida was overwhelming.
Travelers kept a safe distance from one another, and
the trip was silent and surreal. But when I arrived at
my father's assisted living village all hell broke loose.
Dayne was now back in the mountains of Vietnam,
trying to free prisoners of war and get home to see his
beautiful wife and children. In reality, he was
terrifying the elderly residents as he tried to "free"
them from their rooms, and the nursing staff had
resorted to calling the sheriff to lock him in his
apartment. He was scared and very sick, but he was
not giving up without a fight. He had dedicated his
entire life to protecting his country. Even in a
weakened state his instincts drove him to help others
before helping himself.

Despite his age, he was incredibly strong and the petrified nurse refused to enter his room. She wouldn't let me in the facility since I had been traveling, but said if I could not convince him to go to the hospital they would have to take him to a mental facility. The thought of this once proud, brave Airman being carted off in a straight-jacket sickened me. He had been awarded the Distinguished Flying Cross and a Bronze Star for his heroic actions in Vietnam; he served with honor, knowing the personal cost. Although I might have come here as his resentful but dutiful daughter, I was now driven to help a fellow warrior make yet another difficult transition. I called his cell phone and thanked him for securing the area. He let me know he was ready to go and I told him I would send up reinforcements to take him to safety. With the help of some amazing firefighters, I managed to get him to the emergency room so the

doctors could heal his physical wounds and restore

his metabolic imbalances.

The ER nurse handed me a bag containing his

clothes and personal belongings soiled with shit and

blood and said they were going to have to admit him

so I should go home and get some rest. The orange

sun was rising up out of the water as I drove to the

shore and checked into an old seaside motel. I dug his

wallet and phone out of the bag and threw everything

else in the dumpster. Taking off my mask for the first

time in over 24 hours, I proceeded to scrub myself

pink in a hot shower. My rumbling stomach informed

me I needed to go get some food. I found my wallet

and keys, placing them on the table next to my dad's

things while I sat down on the bed to put on my

shoes. That is when I saw it. My wallet and my dad's

wallet were nearly identical. Both were fake black

leather with a little plastic window on the outside

where we kept our green military retiree cards. Both

were overstuffed and disorganized; filled with

appointment cards, to-do lists, receipts, credit cards,

and random dollar bills stuck here and there. Both

were frayed and falling apart. There was no

separation between us; I was no better nor worse than

he was. We were both humans just trying to figure out

how to do this thing called life. In this sudden

moment of clarity, I realized the things Dayne did that

irritated the heck out of me were merely reflections of

the things I hated most about myself.

I had joined the family business to serve my

country, witnessed the best and worst of humanity in

war while carrying the weight of his traumas along

with my own. Like him, when faced with difficult

emotions, I would just work harder to try and push them out of my mind. His suffering was merely foreshadowing of what would come for me if I did not change. In his own way, he was teaching me a lesson I needed to learn.

All his life he had spent preparing for the next thing; every conversation began with his plans for the future and ended with asking me what my plans were. In rebellion, I began to practice being more mindful and present in the moment. That week, as I meditated, I recognized these defenses which protected my tender heart early in my youth no longer served me in becoming who I wanted to be. I made a decision right there; I would listen to the emotions which had been trying to tell me something for so long and refuse to run from these battles of the heart anymore. I needed to forgive and learn to love myself; there is no need to continue to carry these burdens of war.

I ended up bringing my father home with me to Texas. In his moments of clarity, he shares with me memories of what life has taught him and what he values in the face of mortality: making coffee and a hearty breakfast in the morning, the song that reminds him of courting his wife, and playing with the grandkids. On bad days, I just try to calm his fears. I can finally see how my father's suffering shaped my own choices and I have moved past blaming him for my weaknesses. Sometimes, it is difficult to just listen, but through understanding and compassion, I am able to alleviate some of his suffering and in turn, my own. His path is not mine, yet for this brief period of time, we will walk together.

RESOURCES

For those of you who are struggling with

something that you can't seem to resolve, writing can

be a powerful tool to heal physically, emotionally, and

spiritually. Writing helped me through the difficult

process of saying farewell to an important part of my

life, and work through emotional experiences that I

had been too busy to deal with while I was in the

military. The following list of resources were particularly useful in my journey. I have learned through personal experience and research on post-traumatic stress that unresolved trauma can have long-term effects on one's health and relationships. There are many ways to find peace and healing, but what helped me the most was yoga, meditation, and writing. Please, know your story is valuable and you are not alone. By understanding our connection to one another, we will be able to make the world a better place.

Books

Brown, B. (2010) *The Gifts of Imperfection: Let Go of Who You Think You're Supposed to Be and Embrace Who You Are*. Minnesota: Hazelden Publishing.

Cameron, J. (2002). *The artist's way: A spiritual path to higher creativity*. New York: J.P. Tarcher/Putnam.

Gilbert, E. (2015). *Big Magic: creative living beyond fear*. New York: Riverhead Books.

Goldberg, N. (1986). *Writing down the Bones, Freeing the Writer Within*. Boston: Shambhala Publications.

Hawkley, J. (2011) *The Bhagavad Gita, A Walkthough for Westerners*, California: New World Library.

Judith. A. (2004) *Eastern Body, Western Mind, Psychology and the Chakra System as a Path to the Self*. Rev. ed. California: Celestial Arts.

Lamont, A. (1994) *Bird by Bird, Some Instructions on Writing and Life*. New York: Pantheon Book.

Miller, R.C. (2015) *The iRest Program For Healing PTSD: A Proven-Effective Approach to Using Yoga Nidra Meditation and Deep Relaxation Techniques to*

Overcome Trauma. California: New Harbinger Publications.

Pennebaker, J.W. PhD and Evans, J.F. EdD (2014) *Expressive Writing, Words that Heal*, Washington: Idyll Arbor Inc.

Sapolsky. R.M (1998) *Why Zebras Don't Get Ulcers (revised edition)*, New York: Freeman.

Van Der Kolk, B.A. (2014). *The Body Keeps the Score: Brain, Mind and Body in the Healing of Trauma*. New York: Viking.

Waters, E. (2020). *A Shoe in the Sand*. California: Advanced Publishing Concepts.

Internet Resources

Yoga and Meditation Programs for Veterans, Military and their Families
http://warriorsatease.org/

Information and Support for Military Writers
http://www.mwsadispatches.com/veterans-outreach

United States Veterans Artists Alliance
https://usvaa.org/

Veteran Women Alliance
https://www.womenveteransalliance.org/store/Books-c49390251

Veterans PATH Resources to help military transition to civilian life
https://veteranspath.org/

ABOUT THE AUTHOR

True Feathers is Carolyn's debut book and farewell to her life as an Airman. She starts not only a new chapter of her life, but a new book entirely. As a military child, Carolyn Patrick moved a dozen times before landing in California where she met her husband and wingman while attending San Diego State University. Together they joined the family business in service to their country and 26 years later retired each other from the Air Force. Her passion for understanding human behavior led her to study psychology. She earned both a bachelor and Master's degree in Psychology as well as a Master's degree in Strategic Studies from the Air War College. For the first 50 years of her life, the Air Force was her home, passion, and purpose. In 2019 she founded Starfish Warrior Yoga with the primary goal of making yoga and meditation accessible to veterans. Carolyn lives in the Texas Hill Country with her husband, daughter, and two cats. For more information on Carolyn's past and future endeavors check out TrueFeathers.com.